SAINT PETER

—THE—

ATHONITE

St. Gregory Palamas

OUR FATHER AMONG THE SAINTS
GREGORY PALAMAS
ARCHBISHOP OF THESSALONICA
WRITING ON THE MIRACULOUS AND ANGELIC LIFE
OF OUR HOLY AND GOD-BEARING FATHER

SAINT PETER

—— THE ——

ATHONITE

PATRISTIC
NECTAR

Book layout and cover design by Archdeacon Alin V. Goga

Patristic Nectar
www.patristicnectar.org
info@patristicnectar.org

Writing on the Miraculous and Angelic Life Of our Holy and God-bearing Father Peter the Athonite Master Bless

1 In my opinion, it is fitting for us to honor those men from other parts of the world who have performed outstanding deeds by worthily commemorating them through listening to the writings about them, especially since these writings have been published with such accuracy and beauty and they generate a strong desire in the soul for the acquisition of virtue. But why read about men from abroad, when we have our own local example of every good thing, that is the life of Peter? For what reason is it generally unknown, since the contents are in no way inferior to that of the

great saints from all ages who are famous for their virtue? You all know who I am talking about, unless someone is ignorant of this famous Mount Athos and the Peter named after it. He was our very first native and local champion. After overthrowing the adversary of the whole earth on this very ground, he then in this very place became the first trophy of victory over the enmity of him who stands against us; and consequently, by sowing the seed of good works in due season, it eventually sprouted, grew up, and bore fruit. Now it is possible for everyone to know of his accomplishments on account of all the monasteries and cells seen here all around us.

2 Everyone would agree that it is only fair for our leader and guide in respect of such great things to be granted a reward of praise, if indeed it should be granted to anyone. Yet, it is entirely impossible for me to narrate everything concerning such a great man, or to recount, or even come close to recounting, each thing in a worthy manner. For by struggling as he did, he managed to offer such an incredible way of life to God for the rewards promised to the righteous, that is to say, something beyond anything spoken or heard. But my unworthiness in light of the greatness of his struggles, does not mean that I should draw back by exercising silence with respect to them. Well-informed travelers would beg to be excused from any liability in

failing to fully describe those paths they have traveled. Even so, it seems reasonable that such ought to relate their travels in as much detail as they can. Otherwise, we would have to keep away from those parts of the earth and sea upon which we are preparing to set sail and travel, since not every one of those paths is fit for sailing or passable.

3 Therefore, in the same way, I too must now undertake this task and not neglect it, though there are contents in this subject matter whose heights exceed the reach of words. And not merely for me, but it is above and beyond everyone who claims felicity in speech, for, as such, he would have to make, as it were, a rhetorical banquet of all things in accordance with the grandeur of the subject matter. And this being the case, however many there are from the list of reputable men may come to mind, they must readily grant me pardon, since doubtless they stand in need of this very thing themselves, as the debt is a common one, and all of us are altogether insufficient in everything. But I, o holy audience, above all else, take courage in the help of your prayers. For even if this struggle is very difficult, yet by your supplications, the God who raised up our saint to lead such an extraordinary life, who even now is looking upon us graciously from above, can remove every impediment from our feet and keep this homily moving forward, granting a path in trackless lands.

4 And so, appropriately, time has sent into an abyss of oblivion both the parents and the native country from his youth of this great and marvelous father, whose fitting homeland is the heavenly tabernacle. For such things were already overlooked by that noble man while living, being unworthy of his own virtue, and naturally even those who first authored the events concerning him believed they should be forgotten.[1] So he set forth, bearing himself, or rather being born by God, to the place where he took up his abode, whereon he accomplished divine contests, and from where he flew away to heaven. His abode was that conspicuous and, may I say, venerable land, the hearth of virtues, the dwelling place of every good thing, the prototypical and made-without-hands tabernacle of the heavens, that place free from all taint and above all cursed passions, the mountain which properly bears the namesake of holiness. This is the allotted homeland for the saint. And by this name he is spoken of and heard, and in consequence he himself is known, and he bears this distinction among those with the same name, for he is justly called 'the Athonite'.

5 For, if it was customary in Athens for foreigners to claim the city in place of a fatherland after a

---

[1] This is a reference to the first *Life of St. Peter*, written by a certain Athonite monk named Nicholas in the 10th century.

three-year residence,[2] how then did the saint not justly lay claim to the mountain after completing a period of more than fifty years in this place, and in such great struggles at that? If the fatherland, for each person, is the place in which someone might live well, as one of the wise men from outside has stated,[3] how could anyone in any way, either now or in the future, do something better than the exceedingly good fortune of this man? This man who was united to God and achieved divine contemplation, or rather, so that I might say everything concisely, who, transcending human nature and being transformed by a truly divine transformation—if any word could suffice at all to describe the miracle in respect to the immensity of its value—was refashioned by the right hand of the Highest.

6 Now, behold the inscrutability of divine wisdom and God's excessive concern for man and His inconceivable desire to save him. In the homeland of this miraculous father, a war broke out against the Arabs. He, then, as it appears, not being heedless of military duties, fought alongside his countrymen. The

---

[2] According to ancient Athenians law, anyone who had lived a tenure of three consecutive years at Athens could claim it as their homeland.

[3] Aristophanes *Ploutos* (1151); 'Πατρίς γάρ ἐστι πᾶσ' ἵν' ἄν πράττῃ τις εὖ'; Latinized—"Ubi bene, ibi patria"; English—'Where I live well, there is my *patris (fatherland)'*.

foreigners then seized him and, after being carried off as a captive, he was taken far away from home, very far into foreign and hostile territory. He proceeded onward by forced march and was shut up in inescapable fortresses, bound with shackles on his feet, exhausted by lack of food, and afflicted with many things of an unendurable nature. He was in severe affliction and refused a proper life, and, at last, he sought refuge in God. He promised to live only for Him if only he could see the light of freedom and be released from these attendant atrocities. What then did the swift and provident God do? He refrained from haste at that time, and by delaying, He assented for him to suffer those torments more intensely. Undoubtedly, He had the greater steadfastness of the suppliant in mind, since, naturally, after deliverance from oppression, men easily despise agreements with Him, if they are not firmly resolved to maintain them.

7 What happened after that? He confirmed everything concerning his promise by means of dreams. He sent him a dream of St. Nicholas, the great hierarch among the Holy Fathers, to whom he himself cried out most fervently. He had proof of St. Nicholas' boldness before God, both through the vision he was seeing but also by having experienced many miracles from him previously. And the saint did not appear to him just once but twice, harshly censuring the man's

irresolution. Since, though he had promised to depart from the world many times previously, yet in no way whatsoever had he set himself in motion to render the promise in action. And the saint said to him, "For exactly this reason, justly He does not yield, and even I myself am entirely unable to persuade God by making an intercession concerning your future amendment. But if you would listen to me, beseech another helper, a man of great intercessory power before God, that he might join me, so that this thing might be done for you as quickly as possible."

8 Then St. Peter responded, "And who is able to do more than you?" "Symeon!", he said to him, "That very Symeon who happily stretched out his elderly hands with fervent yearning and embraced the forty-day-old pre-eternal God." But then, following the explanation, he vanished away. Once St. Peter had shaken off sleep, immediately the name of Symeon was constantly in his mouth. He did not leave off crying out nor did he flag in supplicating him until he prevailed. For on the following day, St. Nicholas appeared again and ordered him to lift up his eyes to Symeon. And he, upon turning around quickly, beheld an exceedingly august and venerable grey-haired old man, clothed in the high priestly garments according to the ancient custom, modestly leaning upon a staff of gold. He was observing him with grace and kindness, announcing

the good news of his release,[4] if indeed he was ready to keep his agreement with God in action. After St. Peter willingly agreed, St. Symeon told him he was allowed to walk without fear out of the prison to wherever he might wish to go. After showing him the chains on his feet, he then in turn contended in every way that the command is quite impossible. Then the God-bearer peacefully lifted up that beautiful shining staff and lightly touched the edge of the shackles, effortlessly cutting the iron with gold as if it were a spider's web, as they say. And immediately St. Peter was not only free from those foot-shackles, but o the miracle, in a moment of time he found himself outside all the surrounding walls. He was accompanied only by St. Nicholas, whom he saw and who was persuading him that the freedom granted was no longer a dream but was reality. And in the direction of the path, he was indicating the means of supplies, a garden, in fact, with many and diverse trees in full bloom and weighed down with edible fruit. With respect to these, since he incurred the risk of being apprehended, he did not even lift up a finger, as the saying goes, to touch those fruits. But again, St. Nicholas encouraged him, and he urged him

---

[4] Τήν ἄφεσιν εὐαγγελιζόμενον—A reference to the prayer of St. Symeon used in the Vespers service, 'Now lettest Thou thy servant depart in peace...', a very appropriate prayer for a man being delivered from captivity, and perhaps the very reason God appointed St. Symeon to aid St. Peter in this matter.

to pick the fruits without fear. And, after setting forth on the much longed for journey and reminding him of those promises, St. Nicholas then vanished from before his eyes. And though it seemed he was departing from him, yet invisibly he was always with him.

And so, in this way, St. Peter, after seeing the light of freedom against all hope, immediately took the great Paul as an archetype, in that he too was determined not to confer with flesh and blood. And rightly so, since everything happened through God Who arranged things for him by means of a higher providence. For the Lord called him in such a miraculous manner, and this was joined with his astounding zeal whereby he could bear neither to separate himself for a moment nor to cease from abiding in HIs presence. For just as when someone fixes his gaze directly upon the sun and then looks down really sees darkness in everything, so he too did likewise. From fixing the eye of the soul, the mind, unswervingly on heaven, he disregarded everything easily; house, homeland, parents, relatives by blood, different friends. And while still planning to renounce everything and yet not having actually renounced it, he became one with the life of God. The one concern for him higher than all other occupations, was to cling tightly to the divine will and, in this way, to do everything in Christ—to have Christ instead of everything, according to the divinely uttered decree of someone (cf. Col. 3:11).

10 And so, being wounded by a divine arrow, he undertook the journey to Rome, not delaying at all, so that he might be consecrated there more perfectly and fulfill the vow by being clothed visibly in the monastic schema. The great St. Nicholas was still escorting him invisibly, and, after arriving beforehand, since he was already familiar with the city, he met with the pope noetically. For that pope had been sitting on his high throne, as was the custom at that time, being himself a distinguished man and not inexperienced with respect to noetic visions. St. Nicholas appeared to him in the form of St. Peter and explained everything concerning him. Moreover, he enjoined him, once he had arrived, to perform for him whatever he thought those choosing the unwed life should take upon themselves. And so, after giving signs whereby he could recognize the one mentioned and citing his name as he made an end of the meeting, Peter was already entering the city, without knowing of the actions performed by his protector. He decided to proceed immediately to the metropolis, and he had already passed the holy doors and was finishing showing veneration to the holy icons by kneeling, when the pope immediately summoned him and initiated him into a solitary life and clothed him in the garments appropriate for that manner of living. He himself was amazed at what had happened (how could he not be?) and he gave glory to God by offering words of thanksgiving with uplifted hands. And not only that, but, moreover, he added a good and wholesome willingness and, with a fervent spirit, sought a place that would be helpful for his intended purpose. As he came down to the seashore, he met with some sailors, clearly by the grace of God. They were already prepared to depart from the city and were preparing to set out in a little while to the high seas from the port, having chosen to sail from Crete to Asia. And so, he departed with them, having in mind that perhaps he might find some place in the course of the long journey, or rather, even in this trusting in God, who is always efficacious in whatever is advantageous for men.

11 And so, having such a hope, he saw in a dream the Ever-Virgin Mother of God. Standing next to her in the form of a servant was his own protector St. Nicholas, saying to her in a peaceful voice, "Where will St. Peter end up, sovereign Lady?", and she replied by answering cheerfully and modestly, "There is a mountain in Europe, most beautiful and large, in the direction of Libya, advancing very far out into the sea. I myself, choosing it from all the earth, decided to assign this to the monk as a suitable residence. And so, for these reasons I have also dedicated this land as a special dwelling place for myself, and from this time on it shall be called 'Holy'. And for those who take it upon themselves to struggle against the common enemy of man, I will defend them for their entire lives and,

at all times, I will be an undefeatable ally, a guide in
what must be done (praxis), guardian, physician, and
provider of whatever is needed for food or healing, of
whatever concerns the body and both maintains and
profits it, and of whatever lifts up and strengthens the
spirit and does not allow it to fall away from good. I will
secure the approval from my Son and God for those
that might end their lives here well, that complete
remission of their sins be granted them."

12 I know that this word naturally brought
pleasure to all of you. In as much as it
undoubtedly promises the salvation of the soul, so
desirable both for us and for all who believe well. For
when the Mother of God, who rendered the impossible
possible, promises to help, and, not only in this place,
nor just at present, but even in the coming age and not
just in trifling matters, but rather granting exemption
of inexpressible blameworthy deeds, as well as enjoyment of undefiled good things, who in their right mind
would not rejoice exceedingly? But we must proceed
to what follows. And so, after the Theotokos spoke
about these things concerning the mountain, at the
end she added that St. Peter would live there. Then he
awoke and arose for prayer with greater joy than ever
before, and, in his soul on account of this, he was as
though he had wings by which he was rightly made
worthy of such visions and sayings.

13 After a little while, as the boat was sailing near Crete, they decided to draw near to the port for those who needed food and drinking water. He himself did not have a need for such things, in so far as through foresight, from the very onset, he immediately subordinated the flesh, making it an ally. He passed the whole day without food and only late in the evening taking an ounce of bread and drinking water from the sea, and even that in a modest amount. And so, for those who needed foodstuffs, they deemed it necessary to go ashore at the port and, after disembarking, to take care of the provisions of bread and drinking water. Accordingly, just as they intended, so too they did. Then after that, one of the locals who lived in a place that wasn't far away from the port was an extremely close friend of the captain; so, after disembarking the captain went off to him. Upon arriving he saw his companion unexpectedly bedridden, and both his wife and children not sitting nearby and providing as much comfort as possible for the invalid, since they too were struggling with a serious illness at the same time as him, making the horrible situation even worse. Then, the way of life of St. Peter arose in his mind (for it was possible, so it seemed, to make out the virtue of the man from their brief time together). And he said to the sick man, "Oh beloved friend, I have found some medicine for the distress of your entire family", and, turning around, he immediately departed from the house. After returning to the boat as fast as his feet could carry him, he asked St. Peter for the sake of the obedience of Christ in all things to follow him, and he immediately obeyed; undoubtedly God was urging him on noetically.

14 For this reason, he came into that disheartened house of those in sickness, and, swifter than a word, he rehabilitated and strengthened them. For as soon as that man collapsed by severe illness saw this miraculous father, he felt better, rose up, and stood. Then, falling at the feet of the healer, he became completely healthy. Immediately after being healed, he quickly arose and led St. Peter to his children and wife, and, straightway as though he had brought health in his hands, he dispensed it out richly to all. And right away, once everyone was healed from sickness and made strong from being exhausted by dreadful affliction, they took courage, yet they neither knew what to do nor what to say to St. Peter that would suffice in accordance with the greatness of the benefaction. But he, being extremely wary of honor, was in a hurry to return, giving no attention in any way to their praise and attributing the cause of what happened to God. And they even offered money to him after his return to the ship, but he did not accept it, saying to them that it wouldn't be proper on account of the good things done for them by God to give thanks to a man but rather to devote themselves to Him by means of a pure and sensible life and noble behavior and to live according to God, not transgressing what He wills nor ever becoming displeasing to Him at all. For in this way, he said, with the help of God, you will not request healing again, inasmuch as you will not be falling into sickness in the first place.

15 In this way, after setting the inner man in order for them, he allowed them to return to their homes. But he set off for sea together with his fellow sailors, who attributed their fair sailing to the virtue of the man, for, until that point they had managed to sail by a tail wind both day and night and were hoping it would continue for the future. Even so, while they were holding the course and thinking this way, completely unexpectedly, though a strong and favorable wind was still blowing against the stern, the ship ceased advancing and remained unmoving. Though they were 'letting out all the ropes',[5] as the proverb says, the motionlessness did not give way at all. And. indeed, the confused sailors were but a little short of participating equally in the lack of motion, one out of surprise and another from being unable to do anything, for the matter was indeed very strange. The divine Peter, after arising from a posture of stillness and looking around, asked about the

---

[5] Euripides *Medea* (278); Ἰὰρ ἐξιᾶσι πάντα δὴ κάλων'—(literally) they are letting out every reefing rope (i.e. setting sail)

name of the mountain which appeared. And then upon learning that it was Athos, he perceived and declared the reason the ship was being held motionless. "On this mountain", he said, "by the will of God, I am to live out the rest of my life." And he ordered the helmsman to steer the boat to the port—straight toward the dry land. And even as he fulfilled the command without delaying, the boat was released from the bonds and quite instantaneously reverted to being mobile.

16 Truly, is there not amazement in all of this, how the navigable nature and the easily traversed property of the sea ceased?[6] To where did it withdraw and give passage to the ship being pushed by the assault of the winds? And to what place was its nature cast aside, taking on the resistance of a hard body in exchange and restraining the boat in place after the manner of dry land? How also was the easily diffused nature of the wind drawn together in turn and failed to carry away the ship by the pervasiveness of its force, though being walled in by no stronger body? For in mobility, the wind excels the waters. And for the

---

[6] Both this passage and the previous one have a number of somewhat technical references to motion. Since, according to Philotheos' *Encomium,* St. Gregory studied under Theodore Metochites, he would have been quite familiar with Aristotle's passages on locomotion from *Physics* (cf. Books IV, 4-5; V, 2; VII, 2; and VIII, 8).

flowing surface of the sea to become hard just like dry land is a miracle bearing no less glory than for solid land to appear in the depths of the sea upon its being divided (cf Ex. 12–13). Therefore, this must be added to the ancient miracles and narrated no less than them, and God must be glorified for it, for Whom nothing which He might desire is absolutely impossible.

17 But after this, when the crowd of shipmates had drawn close to dry land for St. Peter, they put that noble man on shore at the foot of the mountain with many tears. And he encouraged them by prophesying to them a safe journey and the accomplishment of their purpose, as they had already become discouraged from a lack of understanding. After that, whereas they set out under good auspices, he went forth by violence. Despite landing in an untrodden area, he ascended the mountain and entered into the innermost sanctuary, entrusting himself to God alone, the only One for Whom he was zealous and promised to live[7]—a promise which he was hastening to bring to

[7] The language here has undertones of the prophet Moses and Mt. Sinai. When taken together with the previous section's reference to the parting of the Red Sea, it seems that St. Gregory is subtly, but intentionally, casting St. Peter as a type of Moses of the Holy Mountain. Simultaneously, there are overtures to the language used in the 'Life of Moses' by St. Gregory of Nyssa, in which Moses' ascent is presented as an analogy of the spiritual ascent into the 'inner sanctuary' and 'divine unknown

fulfillment, not only being nearly without food, as is necessary to preserve the nature of man, being in this respect just a little bit lower than the angels (cf. Heb 2:7 and Ps 8:6), but also both naked and without shelter, being constantly afflicted by cold, heat, ice, snow and rains; oh what endurance! He was greater than all other reason-endowed beings, and from understanding the nature of this body composed of earth, how it also weighs down the mind, dragging it down to the earth and not permitting it to have 'citizenship in heaven' (cf. Phill. 3:17), he vehemently caused the flesh to waste away by every means, partaking with exceedingly great moderation of the native plants. By using the mind, making remarkable mental exertion through devoting himself to exactness in hesychasm, he also made a truly divine vehicle of the heart, even another heaven, and a dwelling place for God more beloved than heaven. And that I might say it concisely, he enabled a return of the nous to itself and to understanding or, rather, though it is exceedingly marvelous even for me to express it, a return of all the powers of the soul to the mind, and this by both its own and divine activity.

---

darkness'. St. Gregory wrote this in 1332/3, which predates the *Life of St. Maximos the Hutburner.* Given the instant popularity of the *Life of St. Peter* on Athos, it likely influenced the portrayal of St. Maximos the Hutburner as a new Moses receiving the spiritual commandments on the peak of Mt. Athos.

18 It is impossible to relate with exactness those things that follow. For once the nous has arisen and departed from everything sensory, emerged from the deluge of turbulence concerning such things, and closely watched over the inner man, to begin with (after observing the hideous mask grown upon itself from wandering about in the material world), it makes haste to wash this away through mourning. When it has removed this ugly veil, at that time and only then, no longer being sordidly scattered and in disorder from unstable habits, the soul is led to peace by means of toil, and man truly engages in hesychia and remains in himself. He contemplates himself, or rather through himself (as much as it is possible), contemplates God, through Whom he also transcends his own nature and Whom he beholds by participation, always advancing towards better things.[8] But this happens only if he puts up a fence skillfully around himself from all sides and in no place admits of passage for the primeval author of evil, in order that he not worm his way in and, finding the place swept clean, make it a camp, alas, for his kindred wicked phalanx, and 'the last state of that man

---

[8] This sentence contains two elements heavily emphasized by St. Gregory of Nyssa in the aforementioned *Life of Moses:* (i) that man beholds God by means of participation in the divinity and (ii) the concept of perpetual and unending progress towards goodness.

shall be worse than the first' (cf. Mt. 12:44-45), according to the evangelical saying.

19 But may such a thing be far away from everyone. Once the mind, as the narration has already explained beforehand, has driven out every indwelling passion, then it secures dispassion in the soul. And not only for the mind with respect to itself, but it also entirely converts the other powers of the soul, forcing away all acquired elements. Whereas, in the beginning it drives away whatever was under the seal of the evil one at any time, yet upon advancing toward that which is more perfect, or rather the most perfect, it also forces away that which is under the seal of good; not simply going beyond the material dyad, but even ascending beyond noetic activity and non-sensible thought.[9] And laying aside everything both loved by God and loving God, mute and speechless, according to the written word, passionately devoted to God, then he keeps in check his thoughts about material things and

---

[9] The 'other powers of the soul' refer to the tripartite Aristotelian conception of the soul, which was the most commonly accepted means of expressing the activities of the soul amongst the Greek fathers. The Neoplatonic philosophical terminology of the monad and dyad used to explain the purification of the mind and soul in spiritual ascent place St. Gregory in direct continuity with earlier Greek fathers who had made similar statements; cf. St. Dionysius the Areopagite, St. Maximus the Confessor, and St. Gregory of Nyssa.

forms himself according to the higher forms of being with complete security by entirely transforming into something better by grace, since none of the passions knock at the door any longer. The mind, of course, being well-suited for such things, even transmits to the conjoined body many signs of divine beauty, mediating between divine grace and the thickness of flesh and putting strength in it for the impossible.[10]

20 After this, appear God-like and unrivalled habits in virtue, complete immovability with respect to wickedness (or being moved only with difficulty), and miraculous achievements, both the ability to see thoughts and foresee the future and to speak articulately concerning things that are happening far off as though they were before the eyes. And certainly, the most important thing is that the purpose of these blessed ones is not even aimed at such things. But it happens just as when someone gazes upon a ray of sunshine, that he perceives the particles in the air, even though he does not have this purpose in looking forward. In this same way, those other things are entirely

---

[10] It is important to note that, even in his first work, St. Gregory explicitly proclaims bodily participation in divine energy. This is clear proof that his understanding of this matter predates the later debates and that this teaching did not develop as a result of or in reaction to the heretical teachings but had always been a part of the faith he defended.

joined together with the divine rays, in which the revelation of all things is present by nature, not only of existing things or even what is happening, but even of things that will happen afterward; the knowledge of these things is truly added as a secondary result. The purpose for them is the most excellent perfection for monks, true hesychia or, rather, the fruits of true hesychia which we have said. This difficult thing to follow, explain, and accomplish, although it goes beyond our intended topic of discussion, even so, it has exalted us to whisper briefly just now concerning those things which are above us.

21 Indeed, this man St. Peter, being truly magnanimous, understood his calling and gave himself over entirely to it. His calling was not the pretension of charismatic graces (far be it that such a thing be so, as this great man would never have been enticed by the glamour of such things, since it is not of service to those having learned to undertake the hesychastic way of life, as the narration has stated) but by grace to be enabled to provide a place to restore the inner man and to be well-formed according to the prototype, causing that ancient and incomprehensible beauty to bloom. So, he arranged himself, setting out in this way, 'making ascents in the heart' (cf. Ps 83:5), according to the Psalm. What did the father of murder, the fulfillment of treachery, the one fleeing of his own will from every good thing, the worker or leader of every evil thing, or rather both of them together, the first rebel and he who caused the first man to rebel from God, what did he contrive? And how did he attack him, how did he assail the soul of this righteous one? Knavishly of course, fitting or rather worthy of himself. For he saw this great man was invulnerable to weapons, as they say, through flight from the world and the pleasures in it, by means of which the evil one is accustomed to pillage more ignoble souls. Therefore, this man was progressing correctly toward apprehension of immaterial beings and being enlightened miraculously, as David says, by the vision of the ages, not merely in a dream through imaginative inspiration, which philosophy says is the chariot of the noetic soul for one deemed worthy of more divine visions and advanced toward what is better (for, in truth he had already transcended this imagination). As a result of giving himself over to the radiance of the light on this mountain and driving the darkness into exile, the very one who is himself complete darkness and leader of the intolerable ones was completely unable to endure seeing this man, St. Peter, being brought up from the material world below, from the very place to which he himself had fallen away on account of his wicked counsel. And moreover, he was bringing with him the appendage of the body! So, whereas this man took hold of the higher and better portion, the evil one, however, has not even conceded the very least from what is below.

22 Being disposed of by jealousy in this way, the evil one undertook both to frighten the man and drive him off by abuse. And the first of these abuses was amusing or, rather, ridiculous. For he came out against one person—one deprived not only of arms but even of necessary garments, subdued by extensive periods of lacking food and terribly wasted away from various afflictions present in every limb. Putting on the appearance and uniform of a general and being trailed by a host of bowmen, shouting exhortations and battle-cries, he attacked with boldness against a naked man, unarmed and enfeebled. And he came into the cave which the saint inhabited at that time, calling for a fight. At the same time, all those outside rumbled all around, dashing the large stones at hand against one another, both uprooting the trees and then breaking them; that vain phalanx of followers caused commotion everywhere around the cave.

23 When that great man became somewhat cowardly, he ran to God by means of prayer from his soul and raised an intense noetic gaze to Him, and the wicked one immediately became invisible, not being able to endure for a moment longer. And, again, after a little while, with the entire army having transformed into snakes, the evil one, himself, led them, coming forth not being (or, rather, appearing) like the others, but supernatural in size and dreadful to behold, for he really seemed like a dragon. He raised himself up from the earth, carrying his neck high in the air, appeared to emit sparks from his eyes, bulging his throat, and straightway breathed fire. And he flicked his murderous tongue, extending it far beyond his teeth, being full of deadly poison or, rather, appearing as such. While coming down close to the area of St. Peter, he was threatening from far away to snatch up that undaunted man like a gust of wind and gobble him down.

24 The Saint did not deem it worthy of himself to turn his attention in the least bit at all toward the sight, but, rather, stretched forth his hands unbendingly toward heaven, conquering the noetic Amalek, causing him to withdraw and depart more quickly than he had approached. So then, the avenging spirit felt regret, since everything happened opposite from what he had planned. For through trying to break the continuous thoughtfulness of the noble one and the intensity and exaltedness of his prayer, his failed attempt caused Peter to find an opportunity in that very activity, and so he introduced more vigorous zeal in the saint against himself and unwillingly granted more beautiful crowns. As for me now, considering the situation of this man, I believe he does not come short of overtaking even those who undertook martyric struggles. For whereas those, for the sake of not

renouncing their piety towards God, suffered everything by necessity, he, not being less than them in per-
severance, endured every attack willingly for the sake
of not distancing his mind from God for a moment. For
since in smaller undertakings, he willingly thought it
necessary to endure great struggles, what would he not
endure gladly, even if it were necessary to expose himself to the greatest dangers?

25 And so, in this way, by assiduity in prayer,
he was nearly contending with those
around God in tireless praise, remaining constant in
both peace and war. But the tireless adversary of virtue, though being vexed by his failed attacks, was
struck by yet an even sharper goad of envy. Since jealousy is seen to greatly increase after failing, all the
more vehemently he arose again for vengeance. But
with the outright assault rejected, he thought to turn to
treachery. And so, having in mind to set up an ambush
for the noble man from a place which he already knew
had great power against man and by which, through
cheating against the man's ancestors, it was as though
he tore up the entire race of man by the roots, alas,
and destroyed it. But, since now there was not an Eve
to encounter, for the man had renounced the sight of
women as a thing causing warfare, he came neither as a
woman nor creeping transformed into a snake, charm-
ing and beguiling, and, in this way, wickedly deploying

the destructive counsel. But, pretending to be a member of his family in the world, in order for the action to be somewhat believable, he approached lamenting. Bringing forth the memory of both parents and relatives, of best friends, and however many acquaintances there were from the neighborhood, from every type of age, he wove a lament for him woven with the memories of his fatherland; what an absolutely wretched creature he is and most skillful at fabricating such things.

26 'You have neither escaped the notice of the company of your peers and those outside your age nor will you escape it, because whenever you were among them, you were a cause of every joy and set forth an icon of every good thing. But now you are a matter of unremitting despondency, on account of creating this long absence. Likewise, there is terrible grieving from the children, and not unreasonably, since they never managed to enjoy your goodness, and even more so when they learned that you have not left someone equal to you in virtues adorning the world. What then', he said, 'are you doing, beloved master, behaving in this desert-loving manner, and taking no heed for men by leaving, preferring to waste time with the beasts, walking around in the thickets, living in this disease-inducing cave, dwelling amidst the clefts, and congregating with venomous animals? Perhaps you might say, 'on behalf of living according to God'?

How then did Abraham complete a God-pleasing life among men? What then would you also say about those from him and those after him, or if it is desired even by those before him, preferring to live according to God and not by pleasures, or was that way of life ruined among men? Did they not lift many to virtue by sight of them? And as accepted proof of those contending well, they remained unconquerable for a long period of time, inspired by a desire for every type of good thing and through that zeal being renewed in them perpetually, in undying successions day by day, remaining in this world ceaselessly even as immortals? But you, you will bring your life to an end without a witness in this place, and the labors that will be accomplished by you will be altogether useful for no one, no one among those living now nor of those to come being thrust onward by them. It is as though that person who accomplishes something of excellence, yet does not bring it into the light according to that saying that has been proclaimed, 'Let your light shine before men' (cf. Mt 5:16), did not perform it, as it benefits no one nor does it arouse anyone to zeal; and therefore it harms those who would be improved, and doubtless will be fittingly punished in the future life.'

27 'But if you pretend to believe in the law of new grace and perhaps are forbidding the return journey by supporting yourself with these sayings, I will provide you with that which will confer benefit even from these and I will show you what is profitable. For I came that the judgment be completely explained, since I have not recently been established in your house but from the days of your ancestors am reckoned among the most faithful of your servants, caring for you and loving you so fervently, so much so that it cannot even possibly be expressed. Therefore, oh master, come and show me who, if anyone, you please in this place? How then do you not think lightly of the command saying, 'Let each one love his neighbor' (cf. Rom. 15:2)? How are you persuading yourself that you even love God in this place, since in this place you are seeking only what pertains to yourself and don't even remember this, 'Let each one not seek his own will but that of the other' (cf. 1 Cor. 10:24)? What could you even have as a justification, giving thought to nothing, not the salvation from you to men nor even that salvation returning from them to you as in a circle, in accordance with the written precept, 'whoever leads forth a worthy man from an unworthy one, will be as my mouth' (cf. Jer. 15:19), and 'whoever restores a sinner from delusion, covers a multitude of sins' (cf. Jas. 5:20)?

28 The evil one, as one well-versed in the Scriptures, was harassing him with such verbosity, and it was as though he was showing even now to the venerable one the tree of good and evil and trying to oust him from the paradise of hesychasm. But this man saw through the concealed deceit and, perceiving the scheming and machination, offered him a brief response in order to completely destroy the power of the opponent. Indeed, using a louder voice against the deceitful one, he invoked the cause of our return to what is better, the Theotokos. Then the evil one, straightway as soon as he saw that he did not escape the saint's notice, disappeared, since the mask of hypocrisy was rejected and he naturally wore the mask of shame, he who had shrunk back from coming into an open conflict and attempted to steal the victory with deceit; in turn he was uncovered and defeated immediately, in the first minute. And for this reason, without wanting to, he distanced himself with shame from his activity and by his departure granted the trophy to his opponent who, by understanding alone, easily won a victory against him.

29 So, this St. Peter, being perfectly skilled in mind and heart, gave palpable proof of every virtue in one single conflict, quickly allowing the evil one to understand from experience that he was not ignorant of his tricks. For both through having seen the ambush and not having been swept away in the least by the wickedness veiled in fine words, it is clear that he, if anyone, really has obtained mastery of mind and prudence. For the bait was as though contrived from the pleasant things of this world, in order to soften the harshness of the desert way of life and urge him on toward luxury in the world. Yet not only did he show perfect contempt, but, also, by choosing the painful and afflicted life, he showed he was trained in wisdom and simultaneously revealed courage in soul. Because he repelled that unlawful proposition suggested wickedly by the wicked one and showed himself obedient to God who by nature is Master and Creator, he should not unreasonably obtain the glory of righteousness.

30 But wait, for he who is so continuously implacable against anything good, even then he did not think fit to keep silent. Oh, the mindlessness of he who, when he was not yet even an infant, as they say, knew the passions! Or rather what desperation, for this, when it is disgraced from having withdrawn, is puffed up by empty hopes, thereafter vainly dreaming about a future victory! But the servant of God St. Peter was not so, the crown-bearer shining with such great virtues and trophies. For having offered up everything to God, he also boldly sought help from there for the future. And in this way, since he had been firmly fixed in humility, he was not even harmed in this thought by the victory which came. But, yearning after hope in which there is no shame, he stripped himself for the impending trial through which, by excelling in many things, he clearly showed himself stronger than the temptation, as this narrative is about to show.

31 The one with more shapes than Proteus, the many headed hydra, clever at devising that which is suitable to lead others irresistibly astray, saw that, although this was his purpose for every type of the temptations mentioned, it became instead training for the man in every virtue and for making his way of life more precise, both exceedingly high and exalted. On account of this, he hoped to pillage the inviolate treasure of that man. Therefore, he, who after being estranged from the light by pride and transformed wretchedly into darkness, took on the form of light in order to impart the same blame upon St. Peter. So, he masqueraded like an angel of light (cf. 2 Cor. 11:14) and appeared to the saint with his false light in order to try to extinguish the lamp actually lit from the true and first Light. And so, once he came, he avoided direct speech, eyeing with suspicion that most discerning power of vision. Thus, standing outside the cave, he spoke through the opening by taking courage in the pretense of the words. From that place outside, in greeting the saint he said to him, "Take courage and strength Peter" (cf. Joshua 1:6, 1 Cor. 16:13, Ps. 30:25). Upon carefully considering it, he then asked who it was and for what reason he gave a greeting. Then, he simply said, "I am an archangel of the Lord of glory; I have come to you in order to declare the reward stored as treasure in the heavens for your laborious toils until today and, at the same time, to teach you what must be done at length from here on out."

32 "Therefore, know well that by transcending all those before you in asceticism and forbearance, you will be furnished as is fitting with the greater prizes. For though Elijah fasted, yet he did so for only about a forty-day period; you, however, are drawing out seven years in this place, and you continue on without eating human food. Daniel remained together with the beasts in a miraculous way (with a very few and for a little time), but you for a long time and with many beasts. And if someone should still marvel at the patience of Job, the offering was not of his will, but you, after willingly dwelling in uninhabited places for such a long time and encountering various and sundry temptations, you have not despaired. At length, one thing is yet lacking for you—through associating with men to make them better and after separating them from earthly things to manifest the way of life of the heavens, looking at Christ as an example, from Whom I also have just now flown down. Christ, Who after that anguished stay in the mountains, upon returning, associated with the masses of men, appointing salvific laws. If you are suspicious about my presence, that it has occurred without the aid of God, I will present to you a visible proof of having been sent by God. David, the teacher of His miracles, said to God Himself, "You dried the rivers of Edom" (cf. Ps. 73:15), that is to say, the ever-flowing rivers and not those that appear temporarily as streams. In another place in the Psalms, he says: "You established wells of water in the desert and paths of water in the dry places...from the malice of those dwelling there" (Ps. 106:33-34). And, therefore, as a sign for you that to dwell in this place is no longer according to God's favor, the water flowing beside this place by my command has run dry." And this happened through the one adept in such designs arranging the restraint beforehand by means of another wicked spirit.

33 And so, the sophist of malice offered involuntary praises of virtue and, for this reason indeed, he was delivering the speech persuasively, if I may speak in this way, mixing in a lot of honey with the poison. Furthermore, in order to be more believable, he showed the spring appearing to have stopped as a sign—a thing which wasn't true. But the real person behind all of this did not escape the notice of the great man in the slightest. Of course not! Accordingly, will not copper after having a gold-like luster plated on it, then dissolve after being set to a Lydian stone?[11] In just this same way, the divine St. Peter had the eye of his soul as an accurate touchstone which, upon being purified, always inclined towards God. And therefore, perceiving then the false performance with due measure,

---

[11] A Lydian stone was a type of firestone which was used to test gold and takes its name from first having been discovered in Lydia of Asia Minor.

he quickly brought low that one having risen up and with a few words he sent that imposter far away, saying, "I, myself, am unworthy of an angelic vision. How could it be otherwise", he asked, "since for this reason I both departed from men and will avoid them until the end, knowing myself to be unworthy of spending time with them, being more worthless than them and, to quote the prophet, not a man" (cf. Ps. 21:7)?

34 That one then, according to the apostle having a most appropriate judgment, that is, mad delusion, and not bearing at all the extreme modesty of the saint, changed forms as quickly as he could and fled away. But God, who gives grace to the humble, measured out grace to St. Peter in abundance, not only storing this up for him in the future but foreshowing these things now as security of that which was stored up, even as a pledge. And so, justly, from that point forward, the great one succeeded in living out his life uninfluenced. Just as the peaks of the highest mountains are blown about less by the winds from the procession of the heavens moving together with the air around them, which by coming down through the continuity of space until they are even touching upon them, shows itself more superior than the force and generation of the winds below; in just the same way now, Peter, after running up to the unseen peak of every virtue, that is, humility, was now breathing in and surrounded by the graces of the Spirit from above. Whereas the phalanx of wicked spirits below was fittingly passed by unnoticed and driven away, since their wings were dissolved from the divine fire just as wax melts, as they say about the device in the myths of Icarus being dissolved by the warmer rays of the sun.

35 Then the recollection of the Holy Spirit, after driving back the mischievous powers, also nourished the good servant and sustained with bread he who on this earth was not less than the higher servants by providing for him through an angel on prescribed periods throughout the days. For Although a crow, often viewed as a symbol of a lack of sympathy towards its own race, ministered to Elias, yet an angel leaving off the way of life of the angels, a manifest angel, ministered to St. Peter. To the venerable man, he gave manna, the self-existent and diverse food which has the power to communicate the quality of taste in accordance with the desire of the one partaking of it. And so that great man lived as if in paradise, like in a place transcending the earth, having only some small tokens of association with that which is below and of the earth; living without vessels, without distractions, without things, and, the greatest, without being seen, reveling and being made glad in noetic visions day by day through simple apprehensions of the mind.

36 And thus, living a blessed life for forty-six years in such things, both living for and gazing upon the one true God, being nourished and seen by Him alone, later on, as they say, during the twilight of life, it happened that he was seen only for the greater providence of mankind. There was a certain hunter, who, while hunting, going around in the thickets and searching assiduously for game in order to catch prey in the forest, had a deer appear before his eyes, beautiful to behold, capable of enchanting and inciting the soul of the hunter to pursuit, being both large in size and meaty. So then, this deer was springing forth from one place to another in the groves, and, after coming near the admirer of the game, it would always flee with extreme cunning, being neither in range of hands or weapons, yet nor so far away as to seem no longer huntable. And in this way, for the better part of the day as the deer fled, he also followed; or rather, so that I might say it truly, as the deer was leading, he also pursued. After leading along the man who was hastening forward uncontrollably, both his eye and his mind fixed upon the game, the deer then presented him to the saint. Then, suddenly seeing a man well advanced in age, unwashed, dirty, entirely shriveled up, lacking any type of garment, the hunter turned immediately to flee, having become afraid. For even if such a sight should only produce a small fear, it is able to strike and enslave the soul of a man.

37 And so that one, upon being pierced by a pang of fear, having turned around, was going back the way he came when the man of God cried out in a resounding voice, "I too am a man, o man" he said, "So take courage, be willing to come back for my sake. Since perhaps God sent you here to become an audience of the things concerning me this day." So the hunter, after hearing the voice, at first came to himself and then to the Saint. Through supplication, he investigated the things concerning him with precision and, through this, learned from the beginning to the end about the reason of the saint's zeal for greater things, the fulfillment of this eagerness, the travelling to and ascent up the mountain, the temptations from the evil one, the victories over him, and the multitude of graces from God. After hearing everything and wandering back home, he was imparting this salvific narration to others. Like some good inheritance being passed along and coming down from fathers to sons (by this time a written record had already been made by someone), it has even reached us in conferring benefit. This written record, through refreshing the memory and not slackening in beneficial power, was set down as a paradigm of every good thing for all, as an archetypal icon of an altogether-undeluded life, and as a form of every virtue, unmixed with any evil.

38 Though the narration is hastening to an end, yet I perceive there are still many indispensable things being found left out, of which, by way of adding a little from the things done by that marvelous man after his departure to God, I will give a befitting end to the narration. And so, it is necessary to return again to the narrative for a little while. That hunter, after seeing the man of God, entering into conversation with him, and knowing him as being truly a man of God, or rather to say what is beyond us, even a real angel of God, both an initiate and seer of the things above, he did not give a tithe of his property as in the past Abraham did in meeting with Melchizedek, nor did he promise to bring back something from those things stored up at home, nor even to give half of his property to the poor as Zacchaeus, but he was persuaded to offer himself entirely to God and to the man of God, believing return to the world to be a mistake and having in mind not to be separated from him. Therefore, he said, "I ask this favor from you, your most holy exaltedness, to accept me as a cohabitant, so that being thus appointed I might learn from you. And I will live out the rest of my life safely in a God-pleasing manner, being able to escape the various tricks of the spirits of wickedness and reach God, the common repose of those having lived well—the very God who also admonishes everyone to run to him, promises a deliverance from pains, accepts kindly those at hand, and deems them worthy of greater things than expected. Therefore, become in this way an imitator of the Master, and in no way should you regard as worthless my lowliness, as I will not bear to be separated from the holy sight of you, man of God. For if I should be separated from you, certainly I would live out an unbearable life, as if it were possible to partake of treasure, and a more valuable treasure than the whole earth, and yet willingly lead myself away so to be deprived of enjoyment of that good thing.

39 But this Peter, seeing things afar off, said, "No, do not think in this way now, oh man, since you already have a wife sitting at home, have raised up kin by offspring, and moreover have a large estate able to fill the stomachs of many poor people. Go on then, my beloved child, after returning, and become an aid for those in need, to those hard pressed by need for mercy, and do not fail in being helpful to them, even until you yourself end up in the same lot. For in that case, perhaps by doing well, you will place the yoke of Christ upon your neck, as He says, "since the poor have the gospel preached to them" (Mt 11:5). But be attentive to yourself and be removed as much as possible from both earthly pleasures and cares, striving to retain the remembrance of God in your heart, holding your attention on His name, as though being stored up on a register in the treasuries in the hidden place of the soul. Furthermore, be engrossed in reading both divine books and speeches every day and hour. And if, after having completed a time lasting a year in these things, you should still be willing to come back to me in this way, you will learn more clearly the will of God for you.

40 The great man, having spoken these things and prayed, then ceased speaking and departed from the hunter. After going back to his house and passing the determined year, he set out for the saint by means of a small boat, taking along with him a brother possessed by an evil spirit and two other monks. And so, once they had anchored directly below the place he knew he had met with the venerable one further in on the mountain, he disembarked from the boat together with his travelling companions. And starting from the foot of the mountain, he set out upon the path leading towards the saint. But he was moving along more quickly than the others (for a soul set in motion by pangs of love, perhaps even if it had wings, would not have enough speed in getting to the object of desire) such that, through fervent zeal, he was leaving his co-travelers far behind. And once he had stopped at the desired place, after casting a glance around keenly, he saw the dead body of the great one lying very peacefully, the spirit having left and returned home to the Master of spirits.

41 Then, as though wounded by some arrow at that bitter sight, he let loose bitter cries while striking his breast, weeping, wailing, lamenting, and saying, "what shall become of my wretched self? I have been deceived by my hopes, I have been deprived of the treasure, I have been robbed of my own salvation, and I have completely and miserably lost the wealth I expected for my soul!" He had not yet learned from experience that, although dead, the saint was not at all some small wealth or a treasure able to profit but little those possessing it. A little while later, that demon-possessed man also came up with the monks and, at that moment, immediately began convulsing, and his entire body was whirling and dashing about. He stretched out his hands in a disorderly fashion, was making a disorderly movement with his feet in the same way and rolled his eyes about in a dreadful and inhuman manner. While gnashing his teeth against one another, he sent forth an unseemly noise and some kind of discordant sound from not being able to exhale a whole breath on account of the disorderly commotion of his limbs. And from the confluence of phlegm becoming dispersed throughout his brain, after impacting and mixing with the breath, a lot of foam was coming out of his mouth.

42 But alas, for the one being in such a pitiable state, the spirit dwelling in him uttered words through him to the dead body of the saint as though it was still united with his blessed soul. And he spoke saying, "How have you not yet been sated with your victories over me, oh insatiable one, for fifty-three years already you have not ceased from hitting us, chasing us off, and mercilessly driving us into exile. But you, on the contrary, stood ground just like an adamantine rock, your namesake, against all the various weapons we let loose, and not even now do you appear to be satisfied. And I suffer all this from one having passed away; don't you approach me in this man here in whom I have carved out many inroads previously. Only just now am I dwelling in him after finding a passageway and slipping in. But I will not be prevailed upon, nor will I come out leaving behind the only well-suited lodging for me."

43 After these things, oh the miracle, the one lying down relinquished his deathly and pale appearance in the sight of those standing around, and his skin color changed to something more cheerful. Then, the demon departed from the possessed man, coming forth like smoke from his mouth, so that it is possible to say, with a small change, the saying of David, "When the righteous rejoice (for the indication of this is the change of skin color), the enemy of God disappears like smoke." Is there anything much greater than this in the way of a miracle, either from those of old or in the present? Some from the Old Testament have already raised the dead; such as Elias and after him Elisha who, by means of the former, participated in a double portion of grace. But no one restored himself to life except for Christ, by Whom this man was nearly made worthy by His grace to have arrived precisely at dispassionate conduct and by means of this also unto miracles. If someone were to question one of those who benefited in the same way, they would say that exorcizing a demon is as much more desirable than resurrection as demon possession is more abominable than death!

44 And so that hunter, after being converted from grieving to rejoicing, together with the brother in sound mind and the pair of accompanying monks, carried away the relics and placed them piously aboard a ship. And they made a return voyage via the north side of the mountain. For a while, the ship was borne along by a tailwind, but, having arrived opposite to a certain monastery, it became immobile like a mound of earth, though there was neither a separate wind blowing contrarily nor was the previous wind leaving or even abating. And so, the rowers added their own efforts to the force of the winds with as much power as they had, but the situation was far greater than not only just the wind but also those living. For it was rather the Lord of the dead and the living who was greater, who performs all things in an incredible manner so that the divine end of the life of struggle of the man of desires like Daniel would not remain unheard, that is of this divine Peter. As such, all were despairing together of going forward, so then wanting to examine the stern, after directing the boat straight on toward that monastery, they put into port, and in this way, they bestowed those lovely relics unwilling-ly.[12] But, indeed, to relate the miracles performed is neither timely nor possible.

45 Those co-travelers that came along with the hunter which the narration mentioned a little bit above considered it unbearable to part with those holy relics, and so, with that in mind, they sought to be received and accounted among those monastics, so that they might live out the rest of their lives there. However, after having remained there a little while, they departed with that wonder-working body and travelled onward by sea to Thrace, where again they deposited it against their will. While they were traveling, the time for the morning meal had come about, and the place which happened to be nearby at that time also happened to be perfect for their morning meal.[13] A spring

---

[12] It has been suggested that this was the ancient monastery of St. Clement, which today is located at the site of the monastery of Iveron located midway down the peninsula of Athos on the eastern side.

[13] A pun on words; 'πρὸς ἄριστον ἄριστος'.

was gushing forth at that place, both clear to behold and sweet to drink, some soft grass had sprouted in a circle around it, a beautiful place both for a meal and to recline, and somewhere nearby some plants were growing in the currents of the waters.

46 Accordingly, after hanging the sail high upon the transverse piece of wood extending from the mast, in which they had treasured the dead who was more powerful than the living, they came down into the shade, sat next to the spring, brought out the edibles with them, and were cooking the food. But suddenly, an innumerable crowd composed of people from every age was marching toward them while crying out loudly, making a lot of violent commotion with their hands in a raucous, whirling manner while saying that they were being most grievously injured and suffering horribly on account of Peter. For he was the entire reason for the outcry, being accused of driving them away from many other places, as well as from this one.

47 Near the spring there was a village, named Photokomis; near the village there was a certain court built in ancient times. A company of demons very great in number was inhabiting this structure, and, once they perceived the presence of St. Peter, they were unable to remain in the area. For how could they, being true darkness, bear participating in the light from on high and having a vessel of grace there present? For even as that venerable body was made worthy of this condition by means of the enhypostatized Word, just as the three-day separation of the soul from the body of Christ did not set it at variance with the divinity, in like manner also for those having attained to the Holy Spirit in this life, after they have reposed, that indwelling divine Spirit does not depart from their dead bodies. Accordingly, at that time this also happened there, when through his arrival he opposed the hosts of enemy spirits, forcing them away and throwing them into confusion. And these spirits laid hold of the inhabitants of Photokomis altogether and caused all of them to come forth with Bacchic commotion, but they were not able to accomplish anything by this except to make clear their own departure on account of the defeat.

48 Indeed, that furious crowd of people was transformed into one of both discretion and decorum, and even, before coming near the relics of the father high in the air, the unseemly voices instantaneously were transformed into fitting songs of praise. And since they were so easily transformed from mania, they considered life unlivable on account of what might happen should they depart from this common savior. And fearing reasonably for themselves, they considered how they might suffer something more miserable than what just happened if that body which drives off

evil were not detained. Consequently, though with difficulty, they persuaded those monks bearing the body,
after giving them money, to transport that divine tabernacle "with psalms and spiritual songs." And so, setting up a public and indeed most reverential escort,
they sent him forth and placed him in the village or,
rather, dedicated the village to him.

49 But, indeed, what writing here could enu-
merate the multitude of miracles during
disembarkation? Since the one who previously had
bad sight could see more keenly than Lynceus[14]; the
one who yesterday and before that was deaf, perceived
with ears resounding; someone else who previously
happened to be even more speechless than a fish, set a
sweet-speaking tongue in motion. And anyone having
one or another of their members lame, immediately
regained strength, some had their whole bodies healed,
and others in danger of becoming victims of a terrible
illness were transformed into health in a moment.
Everyone was rejoicing, applauding, and singing songs
of victory. Each of them was conferring not a small portion of their belongings upon the saint. They dedicated
the most beautiful portion of land to him and raised up
a beautiful new temple decorated with valuable offer-
ings. But he does not dwell only in that place there, but

---

[14] Mythical heroic figure renowned for his keen eyesight.

of course also in this land of Mount Athos here, along with not a few others, wherein he is praised and held in wonder and honored with annual ceremonies. Wherefore, I praise him who said 'good men, upon dying, are honored with burial rites by the entire earth', [15] for whom the excellent things performed by them are proclaimed abroad by everyone.

50 To others, nearly to all—I should say that the distinctions won while living die with them. But our great one among the fathers, this St. Peter, even after death is one who accomplished great deeds for all ages. And that which is the greatest of all is that his great honor is not only here, nor even in all the earth (as much as such a thing is determined by the law of grace and in complete accordance with the precepts of the evangelical sayings), but even in the very heavens and is acknowledged by the heavenly powers surrounding God, with whom he himself is now dwelling. For that which happens only for the divine nature, being everywhere present, that man acquired even this, a gift to him from the grace of God; for he is present both with those on earth by means of pious and never-fading memory, while yet remaining in heaven together with the saints from the ages, and is also enrolled together with the angels around God in an unceasing choir.

---

[15] Referring to Thucydides, 'ἀνδρῶν ἐπιφανῶν πᾶσα γῆ τάφος'.

51 In this way, while living, he renounced everything, yet, after dying, he inherited everything. And through departing from the world, even while still being alive, he received heaven after passing on from life or rather had even acquired heaven already even on earth. And through escaping the perception of everyone during life, after disappearing from men through death, he gladdens and delights all the senses of everyone. For he remains steadfast on the tongue of nearly everyone with wonder, has reached equally the hearing of just about everyone, and is set before them as a venerable wonder and the greatest help with respect to disease. And not only this, but he also restores the powers of the soul to strength, through teaching everyone by the examples of his own life both how and to what extent these powers must be used. And in this way, through being a benefactor to all by every means, he is set forth as a common lord of every good thing, leader of virtues, banisher of wickedness, one who takes forethought of everything for everyone, a skillful provider in perplexing situations, and, to say it concisely, a most ready helper in everything for whomever might need anything. Or rather, with the help of God transforming himself suitably for every rational nature, he is at the same time both an expeller of demons, benefactor of men, and co-citizen with the angels.

52 And so, he has set himself before us as a great treasure and perpetual remedy for every type of healing, an example of true philosophy for those who have decided to live virtuously, and a perfect subject matter for those with great capability in words, capable of embellishing their talent no less than he is suitable for being embellished by them. Of course, no one among any of us would be able either to imitate him perfectly or to praise him worthily. Even so, if someone should have the means both to be zealous to imitate him and to praise him, let him do so fittingly, glorifying by means of him the God in three hypostases and one essence, believed in by those of sound minds, Who is marvelous in His saints, now and ever, and to the ages of ages. Amen.

www.ingramcontent.com/pod-product-compliance
Lightning Source LLC
Chambersburg PA
CBHW051335120626
46547CB00016B/2557